HER

IDENTITY

DESIREE S. BRAXTON

CONTENTS

ACKNOWLEDGMENTS

This book is dedicated to my friends and family who have struggled with anxiety, depression, or body image. When I came up with this story 5 years ago, I didn't think it would be able to go anywhere but now it will. For the longest time I was always very private when it came to my writing and now, I'm at a point in my life where I am truly ready to share it with the world. This story touches on sensitive topics so it may be triggering to some. I created the characters specifically for the people who don't feel good enough about themselves and have a hard time talking about the problems they face on a daily basis. Even though this is a serious story, you can still have fun while reading it, I hope that you can relate to any character in the book. When I created Melissa's character, I wanted to show the deepest, darkest parts of her because I knew that people would be able to relate to her. I hope that you can overcome whatever you're facing in life and that the character's stories inspire you to make a change in your lives. Hopefully, when you get to the end of the book, you'll feel a weight being lifted off of your shoulders. I am happy to finally share this story with the world. No matter what you go through in life, you CAN get through it. For more information about this book or anything related to what I listed above, visit my blog: desiree.braxton.wordpress.com

TRAGIC

"Melissa, whatever you wanted to talk about earlier, we can talk in the car. I need to run to the store". My sister just doesn't understand me and I'm afraid she never will. "You'll never understand, no one will". Joanne stares at me. "You're being dramatic." "You don't have to be like mom you know." I say as I walk out the door slamming it shut behind me. As I reached for the door handle the car alarm goes off. "Maybe because I was born first." I rolled my eyes as I get in the car. "Can we just go please?" I turned to look outside the window as Joanne pushed on the gas. "Melz what's going on with you?" She looks at me with so much worry in her eyes. "If it helps, I really don't want to talk about it." We stopped at a red light. "You know I'm just trying to help you." This shocked me because she's never cared to listen to what I have to say so I don't get why she cares so much now. "You never cared about me so why do you want to help me now?" Joanne was speeding. She was going way over the speed limit. "Melissa what are you talking about? I've always cared!" I threw my hands in the air motioning her to be quiet. "Can you please put your seatbelt on?" She always tells me what to do and I can't stand it. "Don't tell me what to do." I could tell this argument was escalating very fast and I tried to stop but I couldn't. Joanne wasn't paying attention to the road because she was too busy looking at me. By the time I looked at the road, it was too late for her to stop. *Boom*. I could hear the roaring sounds of sirens and people who had witnessed the accident all at once. We had a head on collision with another vehicle. Joanne screamed my name to see if I was ok but her voice faded away and my vision went black. Someone called the ambulance and somehow got me and my sister out of the car. We finally arrived at the hospital and they separated me from Joanne. I'm fading in and out of consciousness, I hear one of the nurses say "This one wasn't wearing a seatbelt." You can hear the distant sounds of heart monitors and other medical devices and the voices of nurses and doctors as they are administering my IV and assessing my situation. "Where's my sister, how is she, I need to see her". Joanne screams at the nurse. "Calm down we need to take care of you, you have a nasty gash on your forehead. "No, she is my little sister I have to know that she is okay." Joanne says with tears in her eyes. "Your sister is being taken care of by the other nurses and doctor, but we need to make sure you are okay as well, now let me bandage your wound. You and your sister are very lucky this could have been so much worse. Now your sister is a minor, so I need to contact your parents."" No, I will call our mother, just please let me know my sister is ok." Just then the doctor enters the room, "Joanne is it?" he says as he sits down on the rolling chair. "Yes." "Your sister has a concussion and we don't know how extensive the damage is until she wakes up, she could have some memory loss so we will have to keep her tonight for observation.

Do you want to tell me what happened?" Joanne clears her throat as she scoots to the edge of the bed. "We were on our way to the store and we.... we had an argument." The doctor nods. "She wasn't wearing a seatbelt, was she?" Joanne starts to tear up as she answers him. "No." "Well as I stated she has a mild concussion and could suffer some memory loss and we need to keep her overnight or longer for observation." "I feel so bad because I'm responsible for her... this is all my fault." She says as the tears fall from her eyes. "But it was her fault not yours, you can't put that kind of pressure on yourself. She's lucky to be alive." Joanne nods and wipes her face. "Are you going to stay with her tonight?" "I'm not sure, I need to call my mother." The doctor gives Joanne several tissues and cleans his hands with hand sanitizer before leaving the room. "I'm sure she will want someone to be by her side when she wakes up." Can I see her, is she awake?" The nurse comes back in to finish dressing Joanne's wound and tells her she needs to clean and change the bandage daily, she also tells her she is free to leave and hands her discharge papers. Joanne calls her mom. "Mom, Melissa and I were just in an accident and the doctor says she has a concussion and is unconscious" Oh my God! I'm on my way, what hospital are you guys at, are you ok, never mind, I'll be right there. "The doctor finally enters my room. I was slowly waking up. "Tell me what you remember about the accident." I could barely see anything. My vision was still blurry. "I have no idea what you're talking about." I didn't remember anything that happened, I don't even know why I'm here. "Melissa, you were in a car accident. You're suffering from a concussion." I honestly don't know what he is talking about I don't remember anything from the night before. "Car accident? What are you talking about?" He looked at me very seriously then he started writing down some notes. "So, you really don't know what happened to you?" God, how many times do I have to tell him that I really have no idea what he is talking about? "Melissa you just need to relax ok?" Who is Melissa? "Who is Melissa? Do I know her?" "Just as I feared the concussion has caused some short-term memory loss" "I'm telling you nothing happened to me. I'm fine." He shined his light in my eyes to check them. "That is your name. You and your sister Joanne were in a head on collision and you suffered a concussion and that is why you are having trouble remembering things, but your memory should return soon". He walks out the room and the door slams behind him. The door opens back up and two women walk in I don't recognize them but they seem to know me they look very worried and one has a bandaged forehead.

REMEMBERING THE ACCIDENT

"Melz? I didn't recognize her at all. "Who are you?" She pulls the chair forward to the side of my bed. "I'm your sister…Joanne, are you ok?" "Who is that girl you keep talking about?" I could tell she was getting really upset and she started to cry. The other older lady is just wringing her hands with tears streaming down her face. "My baby" is all she manages to say. "Your name is Melissa, you're 17 years old, I'm Joanne your older sister and we were in a car accident and you weren't wearing a seatbelt." I instantly started to get flashbacks from that night. Suddenly it all made a lot of sense. This can't be real. "Your head went through the windshield and that's why you have a concussion now." Sitting up slowly and wrapping myself up in the covers, everything was coming back to me little by little. This was a terrible accident. "Wait, so what happened to you then?" She started to peel off her bandage to show me her scar. "I cut my head trying to pull you back in." "I…. I never thought you'd do that for me. Why did you do that for me anyway?" She placed her hand on mine and looked into my eyes as she said "I love you, and I'd never want anything to happen to you like this." We were actually getting along. I was starting to remember more about that night. "I remember we… we were going to the store and then we argued… I don't remember anything after that." Joanne began to smile at me. She was actually being really nice to me. I've always thought that she hated me. Soon after our talk, the doctor came in to check on me. Joanne looked so worried about me. I've never seen her like that. How long do I have to stay here?" There's a knock on the door and a nurse enters, "I need to check your vitals, and give you some more pain medication." She checks my blood pressure and adds something to my IV, she then says the doctor will be in to see me shortly. The doctor enters the room, "Glad to see that the memory loss has faded, however I still want to keep you under observation, you are rather small and I need to run some more tests, but you will have to be monitored closely". "Monitored? For what?" I want to go home!" I begin to cry. "Can I speak to you privately?" The doctor asks my mom and they go into the hallway where I can't hear what they are saying. Joanne stands up to hug me. "It's ok Melz, me and mom will visit you every day." I was confused. "Visit? I don't want to stay here by myself." I felt like pulling my hair out. "I'm sure you'll be fine." Mom and the doctor re-enter the room. "I am going to ask the nurse to bring in some anti-anxiety medication to help calm you and possibly a mild sedative. I look over at Joanne. "Yeah she's been like that since she was 11." I grabbed her hand and begged her to stay with me. "Please don't leave me." She gave me an odd but familiar look. "You'll be fine." "I promise someone will be watching you and making sure you eat and stuff like that. I finally gave up and agreed with them even though I still hated the fact that I'd be alone. "Fine. But you promise you'll come see me?" Joanne laughed. "Of course, I better get going soon." "Why so soon?" She gets up grabbing her purse and heads for the door. "I have a lot of errands to run I'm staying with you guys for a while." "Why?" "I have a lot of things going on right now." What more could she have going on right now? I wondered. "Like what?" She looked so tired and frustrated at the same time. "I don't want to make you more worried than you already are." I shook my head. "It's a little late for that." She decided to sit down to explain why she suddenly is moving in with us. "I'm staying with you guys because Eric lost his job and forgot to pay rent so, I need a place to stay until then." She hasn't lived with us since she was a teenager and still in high school. "Oh, but how's your job going?" I realized that we spent more time arguing than actually catching up. "It's fine. I got promoted a few days ago." She smiled. "That's great." I was really happy for her. "Hey, I never got to ask, what was really going on with you earlier?" I don't know why she brought this up. I've never been good with expressing myself. "I'm not ready to talk about that Joanne." "Why are you keeping secrets?" Here we go again. This can't be happening again. "Joanne, I just don't want to talk about it." I could feel myself getting heated. "Well sooner or later you're going to have to talk about it." I realized there was nothing I could do at this point but agree with her to avoid another argument. "Fine." I say rolling my eyes. "I'm seriously worried about you, you're keeping something from me and it's making it worse." "I just don't know how to tell you." It's getting late and I'm sure she really wants to leave but not without getting an answer out of me. "I'm sorry that I'm making you worry but I don't know how to tell you what's going on." "I won't get mad you can talk to me." I didn't want to hold it in anymore. "I've been having some issues lately before the accident. I don't want anyone to worry about me. She looked sad and confused. "Issues about what?" She wanted me to be more specific. "Myself." This is so uncomfortable. I hate opening up to people and boring them with my sad life. "I don't like the way that I am. I really don't. I hate it and some people make it worse every day." She feels so bad for me and that's what I was afraid of. I don't like people to feel sorry for me at all. "What do you mean?" She doesn't understand. "Joanne, I mean that I have problems dealing with myself. I just want people to understand me, I feel trapped and alone." Even though I hated talking about my own problems, I was relieved. "Oh my god, why didn't you tell me sooner?" What was I supposed to do? Tell her before the accident? "I didn't know how to." I think she is starting to put the pieces together. "Is someone bothering you?" I had to sit up straight to tell her this. I decided not to tell her yet. "Don't worry about it." I turned over on my side. "How am I not supposed to worry about it? You're keeping secrets and you won't tell me." I wish she would just let it go. She still doesn't understand. "Joanne this is why I never talk to you; you and mom are the same. You never listen to me or ask me what I have to say about the situation. "Melissa, I have always asked you how you felt. This is starting to get old. It's your fault that you hold things in instead of talking about it." I can't believe what she just said. She basically said that it's my fault again. I'm so done with this argument. "Why would you assume that I don't care about you, when have I ever said that?" I thought we were done but I guess not. "You know what, maybe I'm not understanding, why are you bringing this up now? I haven't done anything to you." This is never going to end. I'm tired of fighting with her all the time. Mom finally chimes in "Girls stop arguing, you guys were just in a terrible accident and thank God you are both alright but you need to be trying to help each other and not be at each other's throats constantly". We both agreed and apologized "I wouldn't be here if I didn't care about you." She said that she'd be back later, so I guess I feel a little bit better now. A couple hours later a nurse walks into my room to check on me. I don't understand how you're supposed to sleep when people are coming in every 5 minutes. "How are you feeling?" the nurse asks. "I'm ok." "You don't look like it at all. Have you eaten anything recently?" "Not since before the accident."

I'm surprised I wasn't starving. "I have a menu for you, let me know what you decide." She seems really nice. Most of them aren't now a days.

THE TRUTH DOES'NT LIE

She handed me the menu and nothing stood out to me. Hospital food is nothing like home cooked meals. I guess I'll just be basic and get a salad since nothing else sounds good. "I'll have a salad." "Good choice." She left the room as I got up to walk around the room until she came back. I had been laying in the bed for hours. Mom started to say something then she stopped, then she started again "Honey, what's going on I'm really worried about you." "You look as if you haven't eaten in days, you and your sister are constantly arguing and you just seem…distant"." "Honey, you know you can talk to me about anything." I don't want to argue with her anymore, I want us to get along". I will stay up here with you as long as you need me to". "But what about Joanne?" "She's 21. She can take care of herself." An orderly brings in my salad and sets it on the tray table. The nurse comes in with a wheelchair and says she needs to take me down for x-rays "I'm a little worried." "Why?" "I could've hurt myself more than I thought." We enter a dark room with very few lights. I was very nervous. I started to panic. "Just relax" she said. I felt like I was going to die. "It's just taking pictures of your head." I freaked out. When we got back to the room my mom asks the nurse what is going on. The nurse says the doctor will read the x-rays and be in to talk to us. I can tell my mom is worried and she feels like they should be doing more. "I don't understand why are you running so many tests if she just had a concussion and her memory is back now?" "We are doing our best to help her. You just have to have patience." She sat next to me. "I'm sorry. I just missed her." She hadn't seen me in a long time. "Do you want anything to drink?" "Yes. Water is fine." My mother looks like she hasn't slept in days.

"Are you alright?" she asked. "Can we have a moment please?" she told the nurse. "Sure." My mother looks at me as she leaves the room. "Are you ok?" I turned over on my side again. For some reason I can't look into people's eyes when they're trying to get me to open up. "Melissa you and your sister have to start getting along." I quickly glance at her. "Why? What's the point? She's just going to judge me, there is no point." "Maybe if you had a better attitude, she wouldn't have a reason to judge you." "So, you're taking her side now?" I had to sit up to make sure I was hearing her correctly. "No, I'm not." She gave me a weird look. "Yes, you are, I can't take it anymore." She started rubbing my hands to get me to calm down. "Calm down." "No." I pushed her hand off of me. "I didn't come to upset you." "I just want you and your sister to have a better relationship." "I just want to go home." "I know." It's time we change the subject. "I've decided what I want for my birthday." I'll be turning 18 in a week. "What's that?" "A massage." "Sounds good." I was starting to get tired. "I think I'm going to take a nap." "Okay." My mom sat in the chair next to my bed and flipped through the channels on the tv. I closed my eyes and fell asleep. "How's she doing?" the doctor asks the nurse. "She's fine, her and her mom are sleeping." "You know you're really good with her." "Thanks." "She will be good to go home in a few days." "She can't wait." "I'm sure." The doctor walks in and out of other rooms to check on other patients. "She's doing really well for someone with a concussion. 3 hours later, I woke up to see that my mother was still by my side. "Hey, I will be back." "Where are you going?" "To get coffee." The same nurse that helped me earlier, walked in the room. "I just need to check your IV." "I have to also check your weight." I stood up to step on the scale. "93 pounds." "You're very small." I hadn't been weighed in so long it was weird to hear someone say out loud how much I weighed. "Ever since I've been here, I haven't really had much of an appetite." "But you ate, earlier didn't you?" "No." I was reminded of a few days ago when people used to bully me." "So, what happened to the salad I brought to you earlier?" I threw it away after she walked out the room. "I got rid of it."

"Have you talked to anyone about this?" "No. I haven't eaten anything since I have been here." "That's so dangerous. Where is the food going then?" Where does she think? "Trash, anywhere that I can get rid of it." "We will have to talk more about this tomorrow." My mom finally came back. "How is she?" "She's fine." The nurse leaves the room.

"Eric, can we talk?" "Yes." "So, what's going on with your job?" Eric sits up on the couch. "Lots of things, I'm already stressed out so can we talk about something else?" Joanne walks over to sit next to him. "I'm sorry." "I have a lot going on myself." "Talk to me." Eric turned towards her. "About 2 nights ago, me and Melissa got in a car accident and she got injured." Eric's mouth dropped. "Wow I'm really sorry. I'm glad you're both ok." Joanne smiled. "We even argued at the hospital and I think she's mad at me." "You and her are both under so much stress right now but you know she doesn't hate you." "I'm going to go visit her again tomorrow." They both hugged each other. "I'd be happy to go with you." The next morning, my mom walked in my room with a cup of tea. "Melissa?" I opened my eyes. "Hey mom." "You look so small." "Mom, I promise I'm fine. "Melissa asks mom if she could talk to her in the hallway as they leave out the nurse walks in with my medicine. "I have your medicine for you." "What kind of medicine is it?" "It will change every so often but for now, it's just for the pain and anxiety." I figured it would be for pain and anxiety. "I brought you some crackers. You need to eat something." I took them from her and took a small bite. They tasted disgusting. I couldn't eat the whole thing. She stood in the corner of my room watching me. I spit out the crackers. "I need you to try and swallow it." The feeling of swallowing it completely grossed me out. "Your body is getting used to eating food again." "Don't spit it out honcy, you need to eat." At this point, I was getting really annoyed with her. "Go away." She was still standing very close to me. "I'm just trying to help you." I quickly run to the restroom after eating the disgusting crackers and threw them up. After that, I climbed back into my bed and tried to go to sleep. The nurse never did what I asked her, she was still in my room. "Melissa?" "Hey, are you alright?" Clearly, I'm not if I just vomited but I don't expect her to understand. "I'm fine." She looked at me as if I was crazy. "You just vomited." "I know that." "This is not funny Melissa, I can't watch you do this to yourself." She was still getting on my nerves. "Why are you so worried about me, you don't even know me." It's my job to be worried you are in my care, and if you can't eat anything you will not be able to leave" "Don't worry about me." "I'm not keeping this a secret anymore." Is she crazy? "Your going to tell my mother?" I know she's not serious. "I didn't say that." "Well that's what it seems like. I thought we were friends." She looks at me. "We are not friends. I'm here to take care of you, not to form a friendship." "What's that supposed to mean?" "You have a problem. I guess we're past the concussion thing but it's clear to me that you have an eating disorder." I really wanted her to get out of my room but with the way this conversation is going, I don't see it happening anytime soon. "That's none of your business, you have no idea what I'm going through." "Well then why don't you just tell me. I heard you and your sister's argument so please just say something." I wasn't going to tell her anything. I don't trust her. "I can't." "Why? How much longer are you going to keep this a secret?" "For as long as I want." "You need to take your medicine Melissa, you are spiraling out of control." Oh my god. This woman seriously needs to get out of my room. "No, I'm not." "Here." She hands me the pills but I was not going to take them. "Fine." She finally gave up and I couldn't have been any happier. As soon as she left my mom came in. "Hey mom." She sits down in the chair on the left side of my bed. "What's going on? Every time I see you, you look smaller." "This conversation is not ending until you tell me the truth. Now." She was serious this time. "I haven't been sleeping." I lied. "Okay what does that have to do with you being small? It looks more like you haven't been eating." I couldn't say anything back to her. "You've been in here for two days, you haven't eaten anything have you?" "Yes, I have." I lied again. "Stop lying to me." She wasn't buying it. "I know that if you were eating, you wouldn't be getting smaller. I started to cry. There was nothing I could say. "Melissa, I feel like I lost my daughter." "Please just speak up. I want you to know you can talk to me." Eventually, the doctor comes in. "Is everything ok in here?" "Yes. I was just talking to Melissa." "Actually, I'd like to talk to you." "Can I take a shower?" "Sure." I head to the bathroom and turn on the water. "What's going on?" "Melissa has not eaten anything since she's been here. She lied to us and her body is not getting the proper nutrition to function properly also her bones are very brittle." "I want her to speak with a psychologist and we will continue to monitor her and if she won't eat we will have to insert a feeding tube"." "Please." She says after wiping the tears from her face. "Was there something going on with her before the accident?" "I don't know." "You should ask her." "I have. She won't tell me anything either." The orderly comes in with a plate of food. "Melissa, your breakfast is here. I brought you a full meal this time." The thought of eating a full meal when I couldn't even eat crackers yesterday, scared me to death. "That sounds hard." "I need you to try." The nurse comforts me. "You'll be fine." I can't do this. Not again. "It's okay." But it's really not and I can't do this again and again. "I don't think I can take another bite." Soon after all this happened, Joanne walks in. "What happened? Looks like I missed something important." She didn't miss anything. "You don't look good at all." "I know. If you haven't already noticed, I have an eating disorder according to them." Joanne looked so sad because she didn't know I was struggling this bad. "Did all of this start because of me?" "No. I need to tell you something I started to before the accident." "What's wrong?" She sat in the chair across from my bed on the right side of the room. "I'm being bullied in school. They call me fat every single day. So, this... this is what all this came from." "You're no where near being fat, not even close." "Whoever is messing with you, I'll take care of them." "Hey Joanne, I'm sorry about what happened between us last time." She laughed. "It's alright. I got over that a long time ago." "Oh, good." The phone rings. I wonder who that could be. "Hey, I'll be back." Joanne says as she leaves the room. "Wait I'll go with you" mom says and follows Joanne out the door.

WHERE HAVE YOU BEEN ALL MY LIFE?

"Hello?" I sat up and covered myself with the thin blanket on the bed. At first, no one said anything. I could hear heavy breathing on the opposite end of the phone. "Hey." I didn't recognize this voice. "Who is this?" "You tell me. How can you not recognize my voice?" This was getting a little creepy. All I can think of is how this person knows me and how he got this number. "No, I don't. So, stop playing games with me and tell me who you are." "Why would I do that? We all have secrets Melissa." Okay this is really strange. He knows my name too? This has to be someone from school. "What are you talking about?" I was on the verge of hanging up.

"You know what I'm talking about. Trust me, I know how to keep a secret." "No, I don't." "You can deny it all you want Melissa. You and I both know what you did." "I want to know how you got this number." I started to get frustrated. "I'm not telling you. You'll have to figure it out on your own." "Who are you?" "You know exactly who this is, and I know your secret." What secret? How did he know I was even here? Is he watching me? "What secret?" "Maybe we could meet in person and talk about it." Is this guy serious? "That's not going to happen." "Why not?" He wasn't giving up. "Listen here, I don't know who you are or how you got this number, but I suggest you don't call here again or it will be the last call you ever make." He laughed and hung up on me. What a creep. Joanne finally came back. "Hey." "Where were you?" "Oh, I had to go see Eric for a minute he needed me for something." "You could've called me." "Yeah but,"

"You didn't as usual." "What's that supposed to mean?" "Nothing. I don't want to fight." "Neither do I. I have something to tell you."

"Are you okay?" "Yes, I'm fine." "I was going to wait to tell you but with all this chaos going on, I figured it would make you happy." She unzipped her coat and smiled. "I'm pregnant." "Are you serious?" "Yeah, I'm having a girl!" All I could do was smile now. "I'm happy for you." "Really?" "Yeah when did this happen?" "I found out a week ago. That's why I never came back the other night. I was getting tested and everything so I'm super excited." "Me too. When will I get to meet her?" "Not for a while." "So, what did you want for your birthday?" "You're really going to get me something?" She looked at me with a look of confusion. "Yeah why wouldn't I? "I don't know, I thought you'd be too busy or something. "Of course not. I'll always make time for you." "Thanks." I felt relieved. "So, what's up with you? You've been in the same bed for a few days now, has anything interesting happened?" "Yes." "Well something weird happened before you came back. I got a really strange phone call." "From who?" "I have no idea. I think it might be someone from school trying to mess with me." "But how would they know if you're here?" "Don't know. That's what I'm trying to figure out." "Did you get their name?" "Nope. He just kept saying that I knew who he was and that apparently he knows some secret I have." "Well is there a secret?" "absolutely not. I would've told you already." "Tell me if he calls again. I will put an end to it." "He mentioned meeting up to discuss this "secret" but I refused to take the offer." "Maybe he sees you around school." "I don't know it's kind of scary." "Scary?" "I mean I don't know who he is and he sounded angry in a way." "Where'd mom go? I thought she was with you." She was then dad called so she said she would be back later." "I'm going to get going. I'll see you tomorrow." The phone rings again. "Hello?" "Hey." This can't be happening again. "Who is this?" "The same guy you spoke to earlier." "What do you want?" "To arrange our meeting." What does this guy want from me? "You do know that I am currently in the hospital. I can't go anywhere." "I can come up there." "I'd rather you not." "I don't know who you are, not even your name." "Anthony." I'm shocked. "How do you know me?" "School." Joanne was right after all. "I actually remember you. You hang out with Jessica." "Yeah she's pretty cool." "I guess. Look it's getting late but you can come visit me tomorrow." "Alright." He hangs up. That was probably the weirdest conversation I've ever had. I fall asleep thinking about the weird guy on the phone and my new little niece who will be coming soon. I wonder who she will look like and say a little prayer that she never has to go thru what I am and I make a vow to protect her no matter what. The next morning, I hear a knock on my door. I couldn't get myself to turn over to see who it was. They had let themselves in. I use the multi-purpose remote by the bed to turn on the light and a familiar face appeared. "Hi Melissa." He sits in the same chair that Joanne usually sits in when she comes to visit me. "So," "I'm happy you decided to let me come visit you." "I see." I sat up straight so I could see him better. He was tall with brown hair, blue eyes, my type. "Isn't there something you had to tell me?" "No." "The secret, you kept mentioning on the phone yesterday." "Oh, that, that was a joke so I could keep you on the phone longer." No way, "But you sounded very serious, almost like you knew something." He threw his hands up. "Jessica..." "What did she do?" "There's some kind of rumor going around." "Is it about me?" "Why would she say something about you?" Didn't he know? "Jessica bullies me, every single day." "I'm sorry. I don't know why she would do that to you?" "We don't get along." "Dang." "She is a horrible person." "I thought you were her friend?" "Well that was before I knew she as so mean to you." "Yeah it was pretty bad." "I wouldn't worry about her she's not happy with herself so she chose you as a target." "Right."

WHO IS HE REALLY?

The day was almost over and Anthony was

still here. I was surprised that he didn't ask about the way that I looked. Normally, that would be the first thing people see when they would look at me. "So, you came here to tell me that the phone call and secret was a joke?" "Not really. The real reason I came was to see how you were doing. I hadn't seen you in school for a few days." "Yeah, I had to take a little break from school." "I see that." "What did you do to make Jessica hate you so much?" "I didn't do anything to her I guess she's just jealous of me." "Did she put you up to this? Why are you suddenly so concerned about me, you never talked to me in school but you're here now?" He got up to come closer to me. "She did mention you being in here but she didn't send me at all. I wanted to come on my own." "Right. I don't understand why you still hang out with her knowing she's a horrible person. Why would you want a friend like that?" "She was not always like that. She's going through a lot herself." "Don't make excuses for her." He smirked. "I'm not. I just know how her personal life is." "Okay. I just don't want to hear it right now." Eventually the nurse came back in the room with a cup of red and white pills. I figured it was time for me to take my medicine again. "It's time for your medicine." I decided to get up to walk around my room for a bit. Anthony sat in the chair just watching me. I still don't fully understand why he is still here but a little company is nice. "I see you have a visitor so I won't take up too much of your time. Your lunch will be brought up to you pretty soon." "Okay, thanks." "How long do you have to stay here?" "Hopefully not too much longer." "I have to ask you a question but I don't want to be rude." Oh, here it goes. "Go ahead." "What's going on with you? You weren't that small in school." "I have an eating disorder." "Wow, I had no idea." "Is that the first thing you noticed when you looked at me?" "No. The first thing I noticed is how sad and depressed you looked." Finally, somebody sees it. "I was just wondering." "I'm sorry that you have to go through this. I'm sorry that I never spoke up when Jessica bullied you. I feel horrible." He was so apologetic it scared me. "You don't have to keep apologizing. I'm glad you're here now." "Great." A different nurse brought in my lunch for the day. I guess this time I won't be monitored even though Anthony is still here and probably will never leave. "Thank you." Anthony turned on the tv, flipping through channels. "You don't have anywhere you have to be?" "Did you want me to leave?" "No, I just don't want you to feel like you have to stay here." "I'm good for now. This is better than being at home with my brother." "Okay, I'm just going to eat so don't mind me." I took the lid off of the plate. This doesn't look good at all. I don't know how I'm going to eat this. "What did they bring you?" "Something that looks disgusting." He just laughed. He doesn't know how much of a struggle this is for me. I wish he did though. I started to think he should have left when he asked because now, he will witness me eating and struggling through it. I attempted to take one bite and I felt like I was going to die. I put the fork down and took a sip of the water instead. "How's it going?" "Not good." This is worse than the last time. I can't do this. Not again. Anthony came to sit next to me. I think he might like me but why me? I mean I look like a zombie but he's obviously not leaving any time soon. "Are you having a hard time?" "Yeah, this happens all the time. It takes me a minute." "I can see that." This is so awkward. I've never had anyone sit so close to me when I'm trying to eat. "I can't do this." "Why not?" "I just can't, it's hard to explain." "But you can talk to me though. You obviously need someone to talk to." "No offense but you don't know me and couldn't possibly understand what I'm going through." He continued to watch me as I struggled. I don't know why he decided to sit next to me. "Why can't you eat?" "It's complicated." "Is it really complicated, or do you just not want me to know?" "I don't like talking about it okay?" "Fine." He pushed the plate towards me. He was started getting really aggressive with me. "I will not eat that." I pushed the plate away. "Just eat the food! There's nothing wrong with it." He pushed it back toward me. At this point, I didn't know what was happening. He turned into a completely different person. Now I'm starting to think he had an alternative motive for coming here. "No!" I threw the plate on the floor and ran to the bathroom. Anthony was still siting extremely close to my bed. What just happened? Did he really just try to force me to eat after I just told him that I'm suffering? "Melissa!" He screamed. I can't believe he just did that. He has to leave. Now. Anthony called the doctor. I locked myself in the bathroom. "I need to talk to you about Melissa." "How is she?" "The same, I tried to get her to eat and she wouldn't so I helped her." "We are trying to get her some professional help, I think she just needs someone to talk to but for now, don't force her." "Okay, thanks." I sat up against the wall on the floor crying. I didn't want to come out of the bathroom till I knew that Anthony was gone. He is crazy and mentally insane. I thought about calling Joanne but my phone was out there with Anthony. I don't know what else to do. After a good 15 minutes, I decided to come out and he was still there. I grabbed my phone and I ran. He tried to stop me but I was too fast for him. "Wait! I'm sorry." He chased me. I ran into one of the other doctors and fell to the ground. Anthony is crazy and I will never forget what he did to me. I bet Jessica had something to do with this. I got up before he could reach me and I ran outside to call Joanne. "Joanne." "Hey what's wrong, you sound upset." "I had a friend come to visit me today but he... he's crazy Joanne." "What happened?" "He tried to force me to eat. He wouldn't even give me a chance, I told him how hard it was and it's like he just didn't care." "Oh my god. I'm coming up there right now just stay in your room." "I can't. He knows my room number, he's going to come back for me I know he will!" "Just calm down and wait for me, I'll be there soon." "Please hurry." I waited for her in the waiting room. I felt like I had to go somewhere Anthony wouldn't think to look for me. Joanne finally showed up and walked me back to my room. When we got back, the plate of food was still on the floor and my glass of water had spilled in my bed. "What happened in here?" All I could do was cry. "He got mad at me because I wouldn't eat and he kept pushing the plate towards me and he just wouldn't stop so, I ran to the bathroom and locked myself in it for a while." "That's crazy. He shouldn't be allowed to come back." "I don't want him to come back." "I don't want you to be alone with him again." "Okay." The doctor said I would be able to leave soon. The thought of that makes me happy. "I was going to tell you that you'll be getting out soon. Are you excited?" "Yeah." "Is he gone?" "I hope so." "I haven't seen him lately." "He better be gone." Joanne started to clean everything up. The glass of water had broken when I threw the plate on the floor. The doctor I ran into walked in. "Are you Okay?" "No." "Who was the guy you were running from?" "A friend." "You seemed pretty frightened." "I was. I was running away from him because he is crazy." "I see. He left and said he'd be back later." "No. You can't let him come back." "Is that what you want?" "Absolutely." "He won't be able to visit you from now on." "Great." "Your doctor should be in here soon," "Thanks." Joanne hugged me tightly. I was still shaking.

WHAT NOW?

I woke up with the biggest headache ever. Joanne was sitting in the chair that Anthony sat in yesterday. My wrist started hurting. I looked down at it and there was a small bruise. I guess it came from me falling yesterday. The doctor entered the room and sat down. I assumed he wanted to talk to me. "Hello Melissa. How are you today?" "Definitely better than yesterday. I have a headache though." "I'll get you something for that. I heard you took a fall yesterday." "Yeah." I tried to cover up my wrist so he wouldn't see the bruise. "I wanted to tell you that your recovery has been amazing. You're doing so much better." "Yeah I am but I'm still struggling with eating though." "I understand. Which is why I'm going to refer you to a therapist." "Oh." "It's not going to happen right now, it would be after you get out." "How much longer do I have?" "Just a few more days." I sighed. "Would you honestly feel comfortable leaving now?" "Not really but I do miss being home." "I get it." "Yeah." "Look, if you feel comfortable leaving early then I will consider it." "Okay." "But you would still have to take your medication daily and see a therapist." "That's fine." "How would you feel about going to a treatment facility for people with similar disorders as yours?" Rehab? "I'm not sure." "I think it would be good for you. You would get a chance to work on battling your eating disorder, and surround yourself with people that have the same struggles as you." "I guess." "You don't have to make a decision right now but it's something to consider." "Okay." "I'll be back to check on you later. For now, I think you need to get some rest." "Thanks." The thought of rehab scares me. However, the possibility of being around people that could conceivably understand what I was going through made it seem almost bearable. I fell asleep eventually. I had a long day, so rest was surely needed. The next morning, I woke up and the bruise on my wrist had gotten bigger. I got up to look for something to cover it up with. It still hurts as if I just fell and it had been an entire day. I hoped that Anthony didn't come back for sure. I don't know how I would react if he did. Joanne came in with balloons and gift bags. Today is my 18th birthday. "Happy birthday!!" Joanne hugged me. She tied the balloons to both ends of my bed. "Thank you." "Open your gifts." She got me a lot of gifts this time. The first gift I opened was a black t-shirt that said "Strong" on it. The next one was a gold necklace that had my name on it. The 3rd gift was a camera. She really went all out this time. My mom even walked in with more gifts. I was so happy to see her. She didn't look as tired this time. "Thank you, guys, this really means a lot." My mom hugged me and looked down at my arm. She saw the bruise. I had to quickly think of an excuse, I didn't want her to know about what happened with Anthony. The nurse walked in and smiled at me. "Happy birthday Melissa"

"Thanks." I hadn't been this happy in a very long time. For once I wasn't sad. I hope this happiness continues. The doctor came in. "Happy birthday. How old are you now?" "18" "ah, I remember being that age. Best time of my life." I laughed because he didn't look as old as he made it seem. I haven't felt this much love in so long. Things are finally looking up. The phone rang. My phone blew up with text messages. "Hello"? "Hey." I recognized that voice. It was Anthony. "What do you want?" "To talk about yesterday." "I don't have anything to say to you." "Please Melissa." "Today is my birthday and I'd rather not talk to you right now. Not while my family is here." "Happy birthday." "Thanks." "Can I come by later?" "No are you kidding me?" Did he forget what he did yesterday? "Please." He begged me over and over but I wasn't buying it. "No. I got to go." I hung up the phone and wiped the tear from my eyes. "You OK? my mom asked. "Yeah, just overwhelmed." "Just relax." I took a deep breath. "We've decided to let you go but you'll have to continue taking your medicine daily." "Like I said earlier, your recovery is amazing and I think you're ready to go home now. I referred you to a rehab center and a therapist that can help you overcome the other issues." "Really?" I finally get to go home. No more hospital food, no more interruptions while sleeping, no more visitors. "Yes." "I'm glad you finally get to come home love." My mom started to gather all of my things. Joanne helped her pack my stuff. I got up to hug the nurse and doctor. "Thank you, guys, you have helped me so much and I really appreciate it." I made the bed up. It's weird to think that I won't be sleeping in it anymore. We walked to the elevator. My dad met us downstairs with the car. I hadn't seen him in ages. "Happy birthday I've missed you." He hugged me. "I missed you too." The car ride home felt unreal. I was finally going home with my family and that was the best feeling ever. I checked my messages and all of them were from Anthony. How did he get my number in the first place? I never gave it to him. He must've put his number in my phone when I ran to the bathroom yesterday. I locked my screen and didn't respond to him. We finally pulled up to the house. My dad unloaded the bags for us and I walked in. "Surprise!!" All of my family was there. I couldn't have been happier. Coming home was worth it. "Happy birthday" my cousin said. She hugged me and the looked at me with a strange facial expression. I didn't have time to explain it to her right now. I really just wanted to go to my room to rest but I couldn't because my family was here. "You are getting so old." My grandma said. She gave me the same look that Adrienne gave me earlier. I guess I'm going to have to tell them sooner or later but not now.

TELL ALL

It was time to sing happy birthday. Everyone gathered around me and started to sing. Joanne stood next to me. My mom passed out cake to everyone. Usually, when it's your birthday you get the first as well as the biggest piece. I don't think I want a big piece this year. I'd rather have a small one. My mom handed me a plate and I went to sit on the couch. Joanne talked to the rest of the family and catch them up. I'm sure they are asking her why I am so small. I know they're talking about me and it feels awkward. "Hey I'm going to go up to my room for a bit." "You ok?" "Yeah I'll be back. My mom could always tell when something was wrong with me and I hated it. She'd follow me to my room and try to get me to talk about it. My room still looked the same. My bed was made up and my room had been cleaned. I guess my mom had been spending a lot of time in here while I was away. Someone knocked on my door. "Come in." It was Joanne. "Hey, why are you up here?" "I was feeling overwhelmed." "The rest of the family is eating." "I'm not hungry." "Are you sure?" "Yeah, I'll eat later." "Okay." She sat on the bed next to me. "Were you guys talking about me?" "Yeah." "Did you tell them about what happened?" "No." Thank god. "Good. I don't feel like answering any questions right now." "They were wondering about your weight." "Doesn't surprise me." "Well, I know you're tired so I'll leave you alone." She left my door open. I got up to close it and laid down. I began to think about Anthony. The thoughts brought tears to my eyes. I don't know what I'd do if I saw him again. My mom knocked on my door. "What are you doing?" "Just taking a little nap." "You couldn't have waited till after everyone left?" "I'm just tired mom." She came into my room and sat on my bed next to me. "I want to know what happened to your arm. Joanne told me you had a bruise." Oh god. I wasn't expecting to tell her today, right now. "Nothing happened." "So how did you get the bruise then?" "I don't want to talk about it." "You're lying to me. You lied to me earlier too, what's gotten into you?" "Mom please, I just want to rest." "Fine. But we will discuss this later." I can't believe she told her. I didn't want to talk about that today. What a day it's been. Later on, that night everyone left. Joanne and my dad helped clean the house. I decided to come out of my room and sit on the couch. "Joanne." "Yeah?" "Why did you tell her?" "Tell her what?" "About the bruise on my wrist, you knew I wasn't ready to talk about it but you told her anyway." I folded my arms. "She was going to find out anyway. Better now than later." "I can't believe you did that." "I'm sorry." "Just don't." My mom came to sit next to me on the couch as well as my dad. What is this? Joanne joined them. What is going on here? "What's going on?" "We need to talk." My dad said. "About what?" "I think you know the answer to that." Joanne said. "You need help Melissa. We will not let you stay in this house and not take care of yourself. You will not waste our food either." "What is this?" "What do you think?" My dad sounded angry. He seemed happy earlier. I guess they talked while I was taking a nap. "Why are you guys doing this?" "To help you." "Are y'all mad at me?" "Of course, not, but I am disappointed." "Show us the bruise on your arm." I felt exposed, this was Joanne's fault. I rolled up my sleeve and showed them the giant bruise on my arm. "How'd you get that?" My dad asked. "I fell." "Doing what?" "Okay it sure does sound like you are mad at me." "No but you haven't been honest with any of us." "I'm telling you, I fell at the hospital." "You were running Melissa." Was Joanne serious? Why is she doing this to me? "Who were you running from?" I started to tear up. I can't believe this is happening right now. "Tell us now." I felt like throwing up. "I had a visitor yesterday." I felt the pain of a huge lump in my throat. "Melissa, this would be a lot easier if you would just tell us the truth." "Anthony..." I felt the lump getting bigger. "Whose Anthony?" "An insane guy she goes to school with." "I could've answered that myself." I gave Joanne a death glare. "You need to tell us the truth right now." I started crying. "He forced me to eat." "I'm going to find him." My dad says. "Did he give you that bruise too?" "No, I fell while running away from him." "I can't believe you tried to keep this from me." "How in the world was I supposed to tell you?" "Look how you're acting." "From now on, you will no longer be seeing him. If I catch you with him, both of you will be very sorry. Have I made myself clear?" I gave my dad a death glare too. "We're not together. I literally have never talked to him until he came to visit me." "Have I made myself clear?" I shrugged my shoulders. "You don't believe me." "I just want you to understand how serious I am. If I see him…" "Bryan, that's enough." My mom looked at me. "Are we done?" "Yeah." I ran to my room and cried my eyes out. "You didn't have to yell at her like that. She's been through so much today." "I don't care Maria. She needs help and I'm done treating her like a child." "Just stop it already." Joanne knocked on my door. "Hey, can I come in?" "No. Go away."

"Melissa, please." "I don't want to talk to you." I got up to look in the mirror and my eyes were blood shot red. I opened the door for Joanne. "Hey, I'm sorry." "Are you really?" "I wouldn't be here if I wasn't. Joanne ran her fingers through my hair. "Why'd you do it?" "I just said I was sorry Melissa." I got mad and started wrecking everything in my room. "Melissa, stop." "Get out!!! Joanne, get out!!!" I screamed. Joanne left my room and I punched my mirror. The mirror on the wall shattered and my hand was bleeding. "Mom, dad, Melissa is going ballistic." They both ran to my room and gasped at what they saw. "Melissa?" I faced the other direction and didn't say a word to either one of them. "Melissa? Answer us." "What it this?" There was glass all over my floor and I bet there was glass stuck in my hand. The pain didn't phase me. I turned around to face my parents. "You will clean up this mess!!" My dad shouted. "Melissa, please talk to us." "There's nothing to talk about." Joanne stood in the doorway watching everything unfold. "I don't know what's gotten into you but you need help." "We won't take no for an answer." "It's my choice. I'm 18 now." "But you live with us so technically, we still make the decisions around here." I couldn't take it anymore. I got up and ran barefoot out of the room and downstairs to the kitchen. "Melissa?" My dad followed me downstairs. He was being aggressive like Anthony was. I wasn't going to let this happen again. He was so angry. He got in my face and I thought he was going to hit me but instead, he gave me a hug to calm me down. I pushed him away and ran outside down the street. "She's gone." Joanne ran after me. "Melissa? Melissa? Stop!!" I kept running. Eventually, I got tired and I sat on a bench. I fell asleep due to exhaustion. "We have to go find her." "What did you do to her dad? You've been drinking, again haven't you?" "That's not your business." Joanne got in her car and drove around the neighborhood looking for me. A couple hours pass and as I woke up to a dark figure that stood above me. When I started to see more clearly, I realized who it was. "Hi." I jumped up quickly and I panicked. Anthony had found me. "Don't leave. Just hear me out, please." "Get away from me." "What happened to your hand?"

"Nothing." "Look, I'm trying to be nice to you but you won't give me a chance." "I have nothing to say to you." "But..." "Please let me go." "I can't do that." "I don't want to talk to you Anthony. What do you want from me?" "A second chance." "No. I need to get home; my family is probably worried sick." "Let me take you home." "I got it. Don't try to follow me." He grabbed my arm. "Let me go." "No. I just want to talk." I saw bright headlights flash from across the street. Joanne and my dad jumped out the car. Joanne ran towards me. "Let's go Melissa now." "What did you do to my daughter huh?" My dad pushed Anthony and punched him in the face. "Dad, stop!!" "Please don't hurt him." "Go to the car." Anthony pushed my dad away and went to his car. I started to cry again. This was the worst birthday I've ever had. "Why would you go with him, after the conversation we had?" All I could do was be silent in the backseat. "I fell asleep on a bench in the park and he just showed up." "You're going to rehab immediately, understand?" "You can't make me." Joanne hugged me. She seemed to be the only one who tried to calm me down. "Hey

Melissa, pack an overnight bag, you're going with me." "Okay."

WHAT ELSE COULD GO WRONG?

I packed a bag as soon as we got home. I was so relieved to get out of this house. "You ready?" "Yes." "Let's go then." Joanne helped me to the car and we left. "Thanks for doing this for me. I can't be here right now." "I know, that's why I had to take you somewhere else." "Thank you." "So, where are we going?" "A hotel." "I'm so tired." We got our keys to our room and I jumped in my bed. The blood on my hands had dried up. "Hey, let me clean your hand off before you go to sleep." Joanne cleaned the blood off of my hand and wrapped it up. She seems to be the only one to care. "Thank you." "Of course." I turned the lights out and went to sleep. I had a hard time sleeping. My mind started to race and I felt as if I had no control over it. I started thinking about everything that happened. Looking over at Joanne, she was sound asleep. For once we actually continued to get along. My cell phone pinged with a text. Who would be texting me this late at night? I opened the message and it read:

Let's talk in the morning. You have no reason to fear me. I promise I won't upset you this time. — Anonymous

I knew it was from Anthony. He's obsessed with me. After a couple of hours, I started getting tired. I slept on my right side since my left hand was still throbbing. The next morning, Joanne woke me up. "We need to talk." The phrase, "We need to talk", makes my stomach twist and turn. She and I sat down at a table in our room. "What was Anthony doing at the park yesterday?" "I don't know. I fell asleep and when I woke up, he was there. I don't know how he found me." "Maybe I need to talk to him." "No.

Talking to him will make it worse." "But he's basically stalking you." "I guess but you don't need to get involved with him." "I'm just looking out for you." "He texted me from an unknown number last night." "What did he say?" "That he wanted to talk." "I think Jessica is behind all of this." "Who is that?" "Someone from school." "I think she told him to visit me that day. She had to have told him to spend time with me to find out everything about me." "That's crazy." Suddenly, I felt sick. I ran to the bathroom to throw up. I threw up everything I ate from last night. I don't even recognize myself anymore. My family thinks that I should go to rehab but I don't see the point. They can't possibly understand where I'm coming from. Joanne tried to come in after me but I locked the door before she could even step foot in the doorway. "Melissa..." I ignored her. "Please just talk to me." I still didn't answer her. I know deep down she doesn't really care about me. She's only doing this because she thinks I need help. I washed my hands and cleaned my face and opened the door. Joanne was on her knees crying. "Why are you so upset?" "Do you not see yourself?" Truly I did see myself. The way that Jessica saw me. *Fat. Ugly.* "I'm not worried about me, I am worried about you." "Did you just hear what you said?" Joanne got up off the floor and dialed a number on her phone. I walked over to the mirror on the wall and lifted my shirt up. My god, I lost so much weight but I still don't feel good enough. Nobody understands how hard having an eating disorder is. The struggle is real. I stopped staring at myself in the mirror and checked my phone. Eventually it rang. The number was blocked. Someone was messing with me. I ignored the call. I thought, maybe they will stop if I don't answer. I was starting to feel sorry for myself. I'm just tired of fighting every day. I'm tired of answering to my family and friends. I got tired of going through this. The accident, the bullying, the bruise on my wrist, Anthony, Jessica, I was mentally checked out. I don't know what else to do anymore. "Joanne." I sat on the couch. Joanne was wiping the tears from her face. She threw the tissue in the trash can and joined me. "You don't have to stay here with me all day, I'm sure you want to get out and do something." "Are you kidding me? I'm not leaving you alone Melissa." "So, you don't trust me being by myself here?" "Absolutely not." I scooted away from her. "So, you're not going to leave at all?" "Not without you." I can't believe this. She really doesn't trust me. "Are you hungry? We can go grab something." "A little." She got up to grab her purse and I went to clean the smeared makeup off of my face. My eyes were still bloodshot red and they burned a little. I guess it came from me crying the other night without taking my makeup off first. We finally got in the car and I started having flashbacks of the accident. I started thinking about everything all over again. I panicked. "What's wrong?" "I'm just starting to remember everything that happened." "It's ok just calm down. Take a deep breath and relax. "We're safe now." I put my seatbelt on this time. My head started hurting. "Did you want to go to a sit-down restaurant or just pick something up?" I thought about it. Did she really think that I'd be able to eat at a restaurant like this? "No, let's just pick something up." "Ok, are you ready to go back home?" Of course, I'm not. Not with the way my parents are treating me. "No." "We can't stay gone forever, eventually you will have to go back with them." "I really don't want to see them. Especially dad. He treats me like a kid."

NOW OR NEVER

Joanne ended up stopping at a place we both enjoyed as kids. I ordered a small plate because I knew how much I could eat. My phone started to ring but I couldn't bring myself to look at it. I always felt like Anthony was coming to get me. He scares me so badly. I swear my body freezes and my legs go numb when I see him in person or even when he texts me. We pulled up to our parent's house. My stomach dropped. My mom's car was parked on the right side of the driveway and my dad's car was gone. I felt a little relief. Joanne helped me out the car and we went inside the house. My mom was in the kitchen cleaning. "I'm glad to see you guys." Joanne hugged her and I just sat down at the table.

She looked at me with an angry expression. She was obviously still mad at me for running away without talking to her first. "How is she doing?" "Ask her mom." She just looked at me and continued to clean. She acts like I'm invisible most of the time and she doesn't even realize how it affects me. "Why are you acting like I'm not sitting right here?" "You didn't speak to me when you came in so why don't you answer that question yourself?" I decided to take my food up to my room and lock my door. "Joanne, you really need to talk to your sister. She has to get help sooner or later, I can't keep watching this happen to her on a daily basis." "I have tried taking to her but she won't listen to me. She has to want it for herself and I don't think she wants help mom." "I don't know what else to say to her." "Me either." "Has she been talking to that Anthony guy?" "Not sure. I know her phone has been blowing up but she doesn't check it. She has terrible anxiety attacks. She had one earlier when she and I got in the car." "Has she been taking her medicine?" "I don't know." "You were supposed to be making sure that she did. No wonder she's acting like that." I placed my food on the bed and looked at myself in the bathroom mirror and I just began to cry. Joanne came upstairs to check on me and she was afraid to come in the bathroom. "Melissa, what are you doing in here?" "I don't know." "You need to eat and take your medicine." She helped me off the floor and led me to my bedroom. I took the same red and white pills the doctor made me take at the hospital. "What were you doing in there?" "Nothing." "You have to talk to someone about all of this. This can't continue to happen Melissa, aren't you tired of going down this path?" I couldn't answer that question. I ate the soup and laid down in my bed. Joanne hugged me and went back downstairs. "Hey dad." "Where's Melissa?" "You're not worried about me?" "I just asked where she was." "In her room." "I'm going to go talk to her." "I don't think that's a good idea, she just took her medicine and I'm sure she's really tired." "I'm still going to talk to her," "No honey, just wait till she wakes up." My mom says. "Fine. How've you been?" "I'm alright."

"Where did you go?" "To get an inspection." "Cool." A rock had hit my window. As I got up to look out the window, my heart began to race. There he was. Anthony was standing outside my house and I don't know what to think of him. I could barely breathe. I had an anxiety attack within a matter of seconds. He just stood there with a blank stare on his face. He waited for me to open my window. What was I going to say to him? I opened the window and I froze. "Melissa?" "We really need to talk. Can you come down?" The thought of standing face to face with him, sent chills up my spine but a part of me wanted to give him a chance. "I'm not going anywhere till you come down and talk to me." I started shaking as I put on my tennis shoes and a green sweater and walked downstairs. "I'll be back I'm going on a walk." "Be back in time for dinner." "Fine." I walked slowly outside and saw him from a distance. He stood with his arms crossed waiting for me. My heart was still racing. I could feel the tension he had as he waited for me. Here we are, standing face to face once again. Flashbacks played in my head one after the other. I started shaking again and I couldn't stop. I didn't even tell anyone that he was here, outside of our house, this is crazy. He didn't say a word as I stood in front of him shaking in fear. Fearing that he was going to hurt me. He had to have known how scared I was because he didn't even blink as I walked toward him. My heart was beating so fast, I passed out. I fell to the ground and laid there with Anthony standing above me. He still didn't say a word. I woke up in the backseat of a pickup truck and I couldn't see who was driving. "Hey, where are you taking me?" The driver didn't hear me. I tapped on his shoulder and he didn't even move. "Hello?" When he finally turned around, it was Anthony. "Where are you taking me?" I repeated this question 3 times and he never answered me. I woke up sweating and my t-shirt was stuck to my back. Thank god this was just a dream. "What in the world are you doing out here?" I sat up and realized that I was still outside my house, laying in the grass. "I fell asleep out here." "Let's go inside. Joanne walked me to my room and I changed my clothes. I decided to get on my laptop for a little bit. As I checked my Facebook page, I saw that I had a message. I opened it and I couldn't believe what I saw. It was a picture of a girl in the hospital with a plate of food in front of her and she looked super uncomfortable. There was a link underneath the picture and without hesitation, I clicked on it. It was a video of me. The video showed me struggling to eat and throwing the plate on the ground and standing in the mirror looking at the reflection of a fat girl in the mirror. The video was a minute and 20 seconds. Who would send me something like this? I started to cry. This looked a lot like the day that Anthony visited me. The strange thing is, he was never in the video so someone must've edited him out. Jessica had to send this to me. I slammed my laptop shut and went to the mirror. I rolled my shirt up to take a good look at my figure and I fell to the ground and cried all night long. I knew that Anthony was acting really weird that day.

INTEREVENTION

My mom walked into my room with my dinner. She found me laying on the floor and she panicked. "Melissa?!" She tried to make me sit up but she couldn't. "Why are you on the floor?" "I was doing homework." "Why do you keep lying to me? You know that I hate when you do that right?" "Yes." "What are you doing in here?" "Nothing." "It looks like you've been crying." "It's just allergies." "No. Something is wrong I know it." "Mom, I'm fine." "You seriously need to talk to me. I will not leave your room until you do." "I'm about to go to sleep." "I checked your laptop." "Why would you do that?" "You haven't been honest with me and I'm tired of trying to force answers out of you so I have to find them on my own." "Did you find what you were looking for?" "Who is Jessica?" "Nobody." "Melissa, lying to me won't get me out of here any faster so you might as well talk." I started to cry again. She must not have seen the video. She looked at the same email that I just looked at before she walked in on me. "What is this?" "Is this what you do now?" "Mom, did you look at the video?" "Yes. What is this?" All I could do was cry. "You need to delete this. Who recorded you?" "I don't know." "This is horrible. I'm going to take your laptop for now and show this to your father." "No. Please don't show him, He'll just blame it on Anthony." "Why do you keep making excuses for this guy?" "I'm not." "Yes, you are and I'm tired of hearing it." "In the meantime, you need to eat." "I don't want to." "I'm not leaving unless you do." "Are you going to force me?" "Why would I do that?" "You're threatening to stay in my room unless I eat so you basically are." She put the plate in front of me and sat and watched me. "Eat." "No." I ran out of the room and went to Joanne's room. She was gone but I waited for her to come back. "Melissa?" I ignored her. I laid in Joanne's bed and buried my face in her pillow and I just cried. Laying there I started to think about so many things at once. None of this is going to matter if I just out myself and end it for everyone. My mom got on the phone and called a therapist. She asked if she could come meet with me and my mom agreed to it. "Melissa?" She still couldn't find me. After a while she got tired and put my food in the microwave. My dad sat on the couch watching a reality tv show. "She needs help and we're going to get it for her." "What changed your mind all of a sudden?" "I always said she needed help. I needed to see it for myself and I did." "That's what I have been trying to tell you all along." "Is there a way you could come over to meet her?" "She's currently hiding from me." The therapist agreed to meet me and she drove to my house. I went back to my room after knowing my mom was gone. The doorbell rang and the therapist walked in. My mom and dad led her to my room. I was facing the window still crying. "Melissa, can we come in?" They opened the door and let themselves in. "Can we talk in private?" My parents waited outside my door. "Hey, your mom was really worried about you so she asked me to come meet you in person." I didn't even acknowledge her. "Melissa your family tells me you've been struggling." I still didn't answer her. "I am." "They told me that you starve yourself and you don't listen to any of them. "No disrespect, but you only know what they told you. You have no right to come into my room and demand answers from me. I don't know you and I will not tell you anything." "I understand you're hurting but it will be much easier if you corporate with me." I turned over to look at her. "They think you need help." "No, I don't." "Listen I am giving you a chance to tell me your side of the story." "What's the point? My side of the story doesn't matter." "It always matters. This is about you not them." "It sure doesn't seem that way." "I can clearly see what's going on but at the end of the day, it is your decision." My parents walked back in. "Melissa, you have 2 options." My dad says. "You can either talk to her and get the help you need, or you can't stay with us anymore." This hit me like a ton of bricks. I have to choose right now. "I don't know what to say." "You need to make a decision. Now." "Where is Joanne, does she know about this?" "We talked to her about it already, she'll be back." "Melissa, your family is extremely worried about you." "Yeah all of a sudden." "Stop interrupting her." "Ever since the accident they act like they really care but I know they don't." I started to cry again. "If we didn't care, would we be standing here right now? Would we have called a therapist to come and try to get you to talk? No." "I don't want to do this." "If you don't get help, you can't stay with us until you do. We're tired of fighting with you every day. You need to make a decision." They weren't giving up and I hated it. This has to be a joke.

TO BE CONTINUED.